Yesterdays Ashbourne

ASHBOURNE.

Yesterday's Ashbourne

A L A N   C H A M P I O N

The Breedon Books
Publishing Company
Derby

First published in Great Britain by
The Breedon Books Publishing Company Limited
Breedon House, 44 Friar Gate, Derby, DE1 1DA.
1995

Acknowledgements:

The author would like to thank the following for their
help in compiling this book: Rod Jewell, Sue Asprey,
Mark Edworthy and Maxwell Craven.

ISBN 1 85983 039 0

Printed and bound by Butler & Tanner Limited, Frome, Somerset.
Colour separations by Colour Services, Wigston, Leicester.
Jacket printed by Premier Print, Nottingham.

Contents

Introduction

MOST of the postcards and photographs in this book are from the collection of one man. F.W.Boden was a well-known character in Ashbourne and an avid collector of many things – coins, postage stamps, postcards, china and cigarette cards. He had an eye for the unusual and many of the illustrations included in this book have never before been published.

Mr Boden was fortunate in having many excellent photographers in the town of Ashbourne. H.P.Hansen, R. & R.Bull and H.Hinge, in particular, liked to capture the more exciting views and events.

Ashbourne is famous for its Shrovetide Football match, but there were many other events which also feature in this book. The townsfolk seem to have made a special effort with their parades and pageants, and their preparation and enthusiasm is clearly apparent in the celebrations for the Coronation of King George V in 1911.

Many Ashbourne men fought, and in some cases gave their lives, during World War One and this sad era is also recorded by the town's photographers. Ashbourne had a Red Cross hospital, situated in the Century Hall in Station Road. Each group of soldiers, as they recovered, had their photographs taken on the steps of the hall, with the nurses who had cared for them.

Ashbourne has several churches, dominated by the magnificent Parish Church of St Oswald's. The spire is a comparatively recent structure, but the church was dedicated in the reign of Henry III and many examples of 13th-century lancet work can be seen in the chancel and north and south transepts. There are many fine tombs and alabaster figures from the 14th and 15th centuries.

There are strong Ashbourne links with the Salvation Army. General William Booth's wife was an Ashbourne woman, and he was photographed on a visit to the town in the early part of the century when he was in his seventies.

Mr Boden had many business friends, and their shops and premises feature in his collection – the Old Curiosity Shop in particular, from where, one assumes, he purchased many of his collectables.

Ashbourne has always been the most pleasant, convenient base for exploring the Peak District, especially Dovedale, and I have included a few views of this area, as well as of the villages to the south. This is not intended to be a comprehensive look at the surrounding area, but to show some of the range covered by Ashbourne's photographers. The first illustration shows Ashbourne's crest, that of the Cokayne family, which dates back to the 14th century.

It has been a particular pleasure for me to take a closer look at Ashbourne. My own family originate from this area and George Eliot (Mary Ann Evans), whose father was the miller at Norbury, is a distant relative of mine. My brother was born in Ashbourne and there are close ties with the Wrights, Moores and Allsopps, well-known names in the town. I hope that you enjoy this peek in Ashbourne's past.

Alan Champion
Derby, September 1995

Parades and Pageants

A soldier on the grounds of Ashbourne Hall after the Coronation parade for King George V in 1911.

Ready for the Coronation parade. A photograph by R & R Bull.

Misses Sinfield, Hawksworth, Slater and Bull, dressed as Sarah Gamp and party for the Coronation parade.

The Emery family preparing to head off for the parade.

Later, in the grounds of the Ashbourne Hall Hotel, the pageant is in full swing.

Boy Scouts pass in front of what is now Spurrier Smith's antique shop in Church Street.

Four church groups turn the corner into Station Road.

Ashbourne's Carnival
King (Mrs Greenwood)
and Queen (Mrs Johnson)
in the 1920s.

The Coronation celebration parade in Church Street.

Foster Brothers, the fishing tackle shop, with their entry for the Ashbourne Carnival parade.

Mr Fred Jones, Mr Jack Stevenson (who was killed during World War One) and Mr George Robinson, seen here in the gardens of Ashbourne Hall.

Williams the saddlers' stall at the 1906 Ashbourne Show.

The 1910 Ashbourne Sports Day on the Shaw Croft. It cost sixpence extra to sit in the grandstand.

The 'arrest of vagabonds' at the Carnival in the 1920s. The first is pictured outside the Railway Station, the second in Church Street.

Mr J.O.Jones & Sons' wagon in Station Street after winning third prize in the 1911 May Day Parade.

The prize-winning wagons are surrounded by an admiring crowd in the Market Place during the 1909 May Day Parade. The photograph was taken by Mr H.P.Hansen whose shop can be seen in the top left of the picture.

Part of the Carnival procession in St John Street in 1909. In the background is J.Osborne's printers, where the local weekly newspaper, the *Ashbourne News* was printed and published.

Churches and Chapels

Canon E.E.Morris, vicar of St Oswald's Parish Church from 1899 to 1924. His grave is opposite the west door of the church.

St Oswald's Church, seen in an early engraving of 1841. The church is known as 'the Pride of the Peak' although it is not really in the Peak District.

The Parish Church showing the magnificent gates which were made by Robert Bakewell. The gateposts each incorporate four skulls and local legend has it that this is a macabre reference to the plague of the 17th century.

St Oswald's Church was restored in 1913 and here a group of workmen pose in front of the scaffolding. They include William Burton, William Wibberley, Charles Bell and William Hawkins.

Churchwarden Mr P.Turnbull is seen holding the refurbished weather cock. With him are Canon Morris and Mr Thomas Edge, the people's warden who had a grocer's shop in the town.

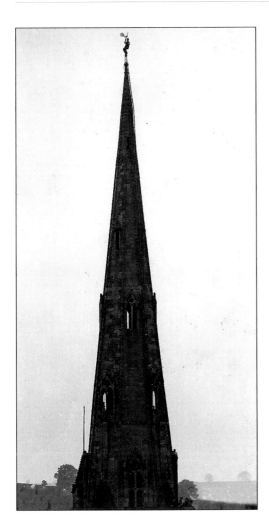

The replacement of the weather cock, 212ft from the ground.

A multi-view postcard showing the main features of St Oswald's Church. Although dated 1840, the postcard was not printed until the early 1900s.

A group of children at St Oswald's Treat on Bradley Fields in 1906.

Members of Ashbourne UDC, and their wives, arriving for the Civic Service in 1954.

Repositioning of the church gates when the road was altered.

Among the Boothby monuments is the beautiful and pathetic sculpture by Thomas Banks RA, of Penelope, aged five years.

St John's Church in Buxton Road was opened in 1871, having been built and endowed by Mr Francis Wright of Osmaston Manor.

Dressed in their best clothes, the Sunday School children prepare for the Coronation of King George V.

The Primitive Methodist Chapel in Station Street, erected in 1894, seen here in 1930.

A view inside All Saints' Roman Catholic church, a brick building which was completed in Queen Victoria's Golden Jubilee year of 1887. The church was consecrated mainly at the expense of Major-General Percy of Mayfield House.

A fine display for the Harvest Festival in the Wesleyan Church in 1913.

Above: The Wesleyan Methodist Day School in 1913.

Left: Young footballers in the Wesleyan boys' playground, holding three of the Shrovetide footballs in 1918.

Ashbourne's Salvation Army Band in 1881.

This photograph was taken by Mr Hansen. It shows a close-up of the magnificent motor car owned by Mr G.E.Gather of St John Street, the first man in Ashbourne to own a car.

General William Booth, the leader of the Salvation Army, at the Ivies, Church Street. Mr Hansen, the photographer, can be seen with his back to the camera, as he takes his own photograph. General Booth's late wife, Catherine, was an Ashbourne woman.

Shrovetide Football

A souvenir postcard marking the Prince of Wales' visit to the Shrovetide Football match in 1928.

HRH The Prince of Wales throwing the ball at the start of the match on 21 February 1928.

The Prince delivering his speech before the game. With him on the bridge are Mr Jack Hawkworth and Major M.Bond of Alrewas Mill, Clifton.

The crowd wait impatiently on the Shaw Croft for the appearance of the ball.

The Prince of Wales and local dignatories.

The original caption for this postcard reads: "Ashbourne's 1915 motto is – 'Shrovetide Football as usual!' This echoes Winston Churchill's comment to the Germans the year before: 'Our motto is – business as usual'." Mr M.Robinson, the printer, holds the ball, flanked by J.Bamford (wearing the bowler hat), William Doxey, the undertaker and William Coxon, the butcher.

Outside the Green Man in 1905.

The action in Compton in 1914.

Some participants in the Henmore Brook by the Shaw Croft in 1909.

Spot the ball here in old Station Yard in 1922.

A ruck for the ball in Park Road in 1908.

A rare view of the ball as six players splash along the Henmore Brook in 1912.

Scrambling for the ball near the bridge in Church Lane in 1921.

The game proceeds along Belper Road and Park Road in 1918.

The Army in Ashbourne

An unnamed soldier from the local battalion of the Sherwood Foresters shortly before the outbreak of World War One.

The Ashbourne Territorials – C Company, 6th Battalion, Sherwood Foresters – on the Recreation Ground.

The funeral, in 1913, of Colonel Jelf of Offcote Hurst in Church Street. He was a member of a famous military family.

Two further pictures of the funeral of Colonel Jelf of Offcote Hurst.

Colonel's Jelf's funeral procession nears the church.

By the graveside. Scaffolding for the church restoration can be seen in the background.

The first wounded soldiers arriving at the Red Cross Hospital in the Century Hall in 1915.

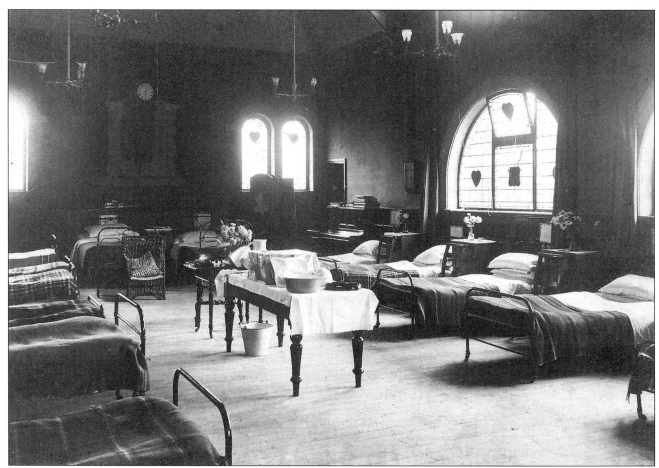

Inside the Red Cross Hospital.

A group of Derby nurses at the entrance to the Century Hall in Station Road.

Wounded soldiers outside the hospital in 1916.

Two young fund-raisers with flags and collecting box on Red Cross Day, 19 October 1916.

The children again, this time the following year with some recuperating soldiers and staff.

The Green Man.

Station Rd.

ASHBOURNE.

Parish Church.

Osmaston Manor.

Market Place.

Church Avenue.

The Ashbourne Red Cross 'Agony Band', well on the way to recovery in 1916.

Opposite page: Copies of this postcard were enclosed in the Christmas parcels sent to Ashbourne soldiers serving in France in 1917.

Committee for knitting comforts for British soldiers, pictured in the Institute, Tiger Yard. This was once St Mary's School.

Presentation of a wheelchair to Private George Smith, who lost both legs during World War One. It was given by the people of Ashbourne. Also on the platform are several members of Ashbourne Town Council. The presentation took place on 10 May 1917.

Armistice Day parade in Ashbourne, November 1920.

The Memorial Entrance Gates to Ashbourne Park.

Canon Morris addressing the crowd at the unveiling of Ashbourne's War Memorial on 10 May 1922.

Ashbourne Fire Brigade, pictured in Cokayne Avenue outside the fire station in 1940. The firemen include Fred Burton, Dick Smedley, Robert Cundy, Jack Sweeney, Frank Wibberley (captain) and Arthur Sherwin.

Ashbourne members of the wartime Auxiliary Fire Service pictured outside the fire station.

A recruiting drive in 1931. Captain Harvey Bond, Mr Joseph Harrison, Mr Thomas Plant, Mr Henry Spencer and Mr Charles Hambleton, all former members of the Sherwood Foresters.

A military funeral procession goes down Church Street, Ashbourne, in 1941.

Shops and Businesses

H.P.Hansen's shop in the Market Place. Mr Hansen published many of the photographs in this book. He also dealt in phonographs and disc machines.

Mr Emery's Old Curiosity Shop was in Church Street, and this and the next two photographs show some of the antiques in stock, and his shop front.

Albert Emery figurines displayed in his shop.

Business must have been good. Albert Emery used the back of this Ashbourne postcard to inform clients of his move to larger premises.

Right: Albert Emery outside his new shop in Church Street.

Two pictures of Cannon's Stables at the White Hart Hotel. They ran trips to Dovedale and also had horses for hire.

St John's Pharmacy, owned by Thomas Wardle, manufacturer of aerated waters and patent medicines.

The Osborne family outside their house, the Ivies, in Church Street in 1920. Mr Osborne, the chemist, was a famous inventor of patent medicines. His son, seen here wearing a trilby hat, was a local solicitor.

C.Lee & Son, jewellers, whose premises
were then in the Market Place.

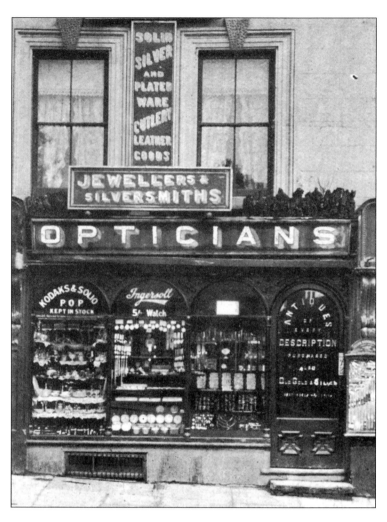

Taylor's shop in Station Street.

Mellor's grocery shop in 1908. It later became the Mart.

A familiar sight in Ashbourne, Spencer's Dining Rooms in the Market Place, pictured here in the early part of this century.

Lumbard's Yard, near Crompton Street, in 1935.

Entrance to the Stag and Pheasant Yard.

The Crompton Carriage Works of Edward Lumbar. Many of the prize winners in the May Day parades would have been made here.

Scenes and Characters

The National School treat in 1906,
on the way to Bradley Fields.

Mr Emery, owner
of the Old
Curiosity Shop,
was also an
auctioneer.

The unusual and famous sign, 'Green Man and Black's Head', in St John Street, pictured in 1928.

Mr A.M.Winter, for many years manager of the Ashbourne branch of the Westminster Bank, pictured in his Freemason regalia. He was Grand Master of the Ashbourne St Oswald Lodge in 1893.

A framed portrait of Mr G.H.Elkes was presented to him by the Ashbourne Dove Valley Lodge of the Freemasons in 1908, before his move to Uttoxeter.

Children outside the Red Lion Inn in the Market Place.

Ashbourne Town Hall, Market Place, in 1915.

Two different views of the Market Place, separated by 50 years.

Looking across the grounds to Ashbourne Hall, which at this time was an hotel. Part of the hall is now the local library.

A motor tricycle leaving the back entrance of the Hall Hotel in Hall Lane.

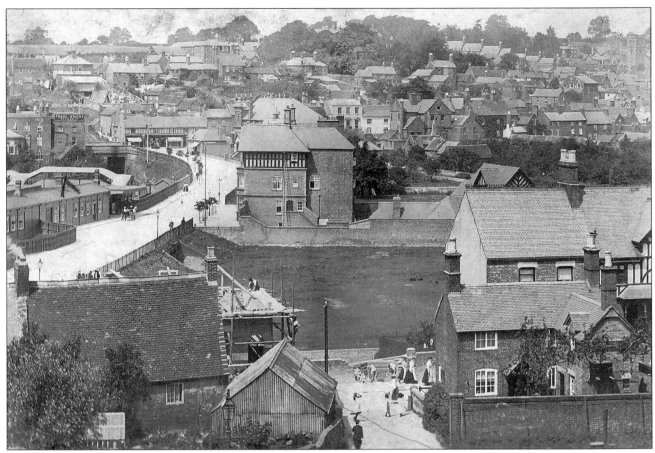

The construction of Station Street, pictured on this postcard mailed in 1904, shows the new railway station and the Station Hotel.

A train arriving at Ashbourne Railway Station in 1950.

Station Street, looking from Clifton Road in 1918.

Nestlé's sidings on Clifton Road in 1926.

The new Grammar School in 1911.

The Grammar School fair in 1930, with the headmaster, Major F.Ball, pictured.

Church Street, looking down to the Green Man in 1912.

A Parliamentary election meeting held by Mr E.Himners in 1910.

St John Street in 1934, looking towards St Oswald's Church.

Much of Ashbourne has remained unchanged, but this view of Compton is barely recognisable, with modern buildings all but hiding the bridge.

The Almshouses in Church Street and two of their occupants, Mr Jack Keeling, a chimney sweep, and his wife.

A rare view inside the Workhouse on Churchbanks. Jane Moon, in her 90th year, enjoys a clay pipe.

Ashbourne's new fire engine. Built by John Morris & Sons of Salford, it had been on show at the British Empire Exhibition at Wembley the previous year, 1924.

The Town band at Bradley Pastures at the turn of the century. Bandmaster Charles Salt can be seen in the choir on the front row.

Ashbourne Corset Factory Bowling Club Cup winners. Amongst those pictured are Edward Wibberley, Jim Hopkins, Herbert Sweeney, Bert Breeze, William Cox, Alf Asher (holding the cup) and Peter Hoptroff.

St Oswald's Hospital in Belle Vue Road, floodlit in 1934.

Surrounding Villages

Dovedale was as popular in Edwardian times as it is today. The Peveril of the Peak Hotel (above), a popular starting point for walkers into Dovedale while the distinctive peak of Thorpe Cloud (below) commands wonderful views along the valley.

The New Inn Hotel on Buxton Road in 1924.

Donkey rides were a tourist attraction for many years. This view was taken in 1907.

William Burton of King Street, pictured with his donkeys going to Dovedale in 1945.

The picturesque village of Osmaston. This view near the Village Hall was captured by
R & R Bull in 1905.

Osmaston Manor, near Ashbourne, was an early Victorian building which was later owned by Sir Ian Walker-Oakover. It was demolished in 1966.

Mrs Ann Barlow, sitting outside her cottage in Osmaston in 1905.

The Shoulder of Mutton Inn, Osmaston. When this photograph was taken the landlord was Alfred Coxon, and he used it for a Christmas card in 1914.

The new cottages in Osmaston, built to fit in with the many thatched and half-timbered dwellings in the village.

A group standing above the water-wheel in the grounds of Osmaston Hall.

Shirley Bank, near Ashbourne, pictured in 1903, by the same photographer – P.R.Webster – who took the previous view.

St Michael's Church, Shirley, pictured on a postcard sent to a Rotherham address in 1904. The gates have been replaced and the tower now boasts a clock.

Shirley Vicarage faces the church across a shallow valley. The vicarage is now the residence of Lord Tamworth.

Snelston Vicarage, *c.* 1905.

Clifton Parish Church choir in 1928, proudly displaying the banner won in the Colwich Art Society contest. In this picture are S.Coates, the organist, on the back row, and Ted Dean, holding the banner.

One of Derbyshire's most ancient traditions of well-dressing is shown here in a postcard taken from the *Mirror* newspaper in 1837.

Many towns and villages dress wells. This one is at Tissington.

St Leonard's Church, Thorpe, pictured on a postcard published by R & R Bull. Today, trees almost obscure this view.

A large congregation is present for the opening of Clifton Cemetery.

A Wyaston United football team of bygone days. Back row (left to right): Williamson, Mr Affleck senior, Johnson, Connell, J.Gamble, Mr Gamble senior, Cresswell. Middle row: Stanley, Affleck, Allsop. Front row: Parker, Hill, Keeling, Atkin, Gallimore.

Teachers and pupils of Swinscoe School in 1910.